TYPES OF MODERN
INDIAN BUILDINGS

TYPES OF MODERN
INDIAN BUILDINGS:

AT

DELHI, AGRA, ALLAHABAD, LUCKNOW, AJMER, BHOPAL, BIKANER, GWALIOR, JAIPUR, JODHPUR AND UDAIPUR

SANDERSON GORDON

GYAN

Published by

GYAN

Gyan Publishing House
5, Ansari Road
Daryaganj, New Delhi-110002
Phone: 011-47034999, 9811692060
E-mail: books@gyanbooks.com

Distribution Network
gyanbooks.com
India, USA, Canada, UK, Australia

ISBN: 978-93-6433-072-5 (PB)

First Published, 1918

2nd Impression 2024

Printed at: Gyan Press, Delhi.

TYPES OF MODERN INDIAN BUILDINGS
Author: SANDERSON GORDON

Frontispiece.,

A TYPICAL BHOPAL HOUSE WITH SHOPS BELOW.

Photo.-Mechl. Dept., Thomason College, Roorkee.

TYPES OF MODERN INDIAN

BUILDINGS

AT

Delhi, Agra, Allahabad, Lucknow, Ajmer, Bhopal, Bikanir, Gwalior, Jaipur, Jodhpur and Udaipur,

With notes on the craftsmen employed on their design and execution.

ALLAHABAD:

PRINTED BY F. LUKER, SUPDT., GOVERNMENT PRESS, UNITED PROVINCES.

1913.

Price, Rs. 9 (13*s*. 6*d*.)

PREFACE.

This volume is the result of certain inquiries made by Mr. Gordon Sanderson, Superintendent, Muhammadan and British Monuments, Northern Circle, Agra, under the direction of Dr. J. H. Marshall, C.I.E., Litt. D., F.S.A., Director General of Archaeology in India.

The photographs were collected by Mr. Sanderson and he has written the descriptive notes which accompany them. Mr. J. Begg, F.R.I.B.A., Consulting Architect to the Government of India has also kindly furnished an introductory note on the development of Indian Architecture.

The opinions expressed by Mr. Begg and Mr. Sanderson are personal to themselves and the Government of India is in no way committed to the approval of their views.

CONTENTS.

LIST OF PLATES.

APPENDIX.

LIST OF PLATES.

"Architecture in India is still a living Art, practised on the principles which caused its wonderful development in Europe in the 12th and 13th centuries ; and there consequently, and there alone, the student of architecture has a chance of seeing the real principles of the art in action." (*Fergusson.*)

Note on the Development of Indian Architecture.

INDIA with respect to architecture, while she is in a similar position to that of other nations in possessing an impressive heritage in the monuments of the past, is yet unlike them in two remarkable particulars. First, in spite of the incentive such a heritage might have afforded, she has hardly begun as a nation to develop a modern architecture. Second, she possesses, on the other hand, another heritage, that unique and wonderful thing, a still living style-tradition.

It is not difficult to understand the reason for the first of these two peculiarities. India's position in modern civilization has been the result of a special process. She has been under tutelage, and has shewn herself apt to come into line in most phases of the modern world's activity to which her attention has been directed. But her crafts have been chiefly engaged with the things she most needed to enable her civilization to expand, railways, irrigation and the like. It is of comparatively recent years only that architecture has received serious attention from the guardians of the country, and that attention has hardly yet begun to be shared to any appreciable extent by Indians themselves. India is not yet giving the best of her brains to it. Youths of the class that is producing plenty of lawyers and doctors are hardly yet seeking careers in the study and practice of architecture.

At the moment, however, a wave of enthusiasm for a national architecture is passing over India. Public opinion may be said to be calling out for a supply of it, and when public opinion in India calls out for anything, it generally looks to Government as a sort of Universal Provider, who can at once reach down the article required from the shelf on which it is presumed to be reposing. But surely it is not Government merely, but more particularly the nation itself which should supply national art. The present wave of aspiration is a good thing so far as it goes, and it behoves us all to help it on. But it rests with Indians themselves to see that it goes far enough, that it does not stop short with enthusiasms and demands, but concretes itself into men and work.

A useful outcome, and one which may well stand for an earnest of Government's sympathy in the matter, has been the publication of this collection of photographs. And that brings me to the second great fact which to-day differentiates India's position in architecture from that of other countries. These photographs should amply prove to anyone who might have a doubt on the point the fact of the survival to the present day of a living tradition. To some this may appear to be no more than a trace; a shoot which we find in the more retired by-ways of the land. How it comes that it is a shoot and not a sturdy tree, and how merely in the by-ways and not in the high-ways it will avail us little to speculate. There it is.—I need not add any critical comments to those of Mr. Sanderson whose notes amply cover the ground, and call attention in a sympathetic manner to the salient points in the work illustrated. In judging of such work the architect must, as Mr. Sanderson (himself an architect) has done, be careful to avoid too critical a standpoint with regard to much of it, to remember who and what these craftsmen-designers are, as well as the educational advantages they have not.

To the severe critic it will certainly appear that the style, as represented by these modern buildings, has tended to decay from the state in which it is seen in the old examples. It must be admitted that it has become rather perfunctory, even mechanical, (as hinted at, for instance, by the "pattern-book" shewn on plate 8). It has also shewn a tendency towards over-elaboration. But in the circumstances is this decadence to be wondered at?. The kindest, as well as the truest summing up of the case is to say that the art, though still living, is dormant, and the question with regard to it is this—is it worth re-awakening? Should we allow it to die the natural death that from one cause or another has overtaken nearly all similar art traditions in other countries, or should we try to give it a new lease of life?

The question is momentous, full of difficulty, not to be hastily dealt with, impossible to be answered without a very careful reviewing of the whole ground, yet imperatively demanding an immediate answer. The time has come for us to think out and declare a definite architectural policy for India; just as we have thought out a railway policy and an educational policy. That is the message which the present burst of public interest in the question of Indian architecture seems intended to convey.

I think the answer must be that the living tradition is an artistic asset of such incalculable value that we cannot afford to allow it to die out; that it is well worth re-awakening, even though the complete process should be lengthy and interim results not acceptable, may be, to all. The architecture may take a hundred years to find itself, and still be "worth while." That it can be so developed, that it can be made to supply all the complex needs of modern India in a manner in conformity at once with sound business principles and with the canons of true art, I have no shadow of doubt.

It is easy to try to brush aside this line of argument by the use of a few witty opprobrious epithets. It is easy to call names, and architectural criticism, so-called, is peculiarly rich in them. One can well imagine that the beginnings of, say, the Italian renaissance were not unattended by vituperation. The earlier products of that movement were probably considered to be illegitimate by the orthodox gothicists of the day. "Sham classicism" they would be called. And while I have no intention of likening the re-awakening of Indian art to the Italian renaissance, still I hold that the former has in it inherent potentialities of which it is impossible to foresee (as it is ungenerous to disparage beforehand) the ultimate outcome. The truth is a great deal of unnecessary apprehension and misunderstanding befog the idea of a developed Indian style. The advocates of a Western manner propose (quite properly) to adapt their style to the conditions of the country. That is, surely, to Orientalize it. But would not to do so be equally likely to result in a "bastard product" as would, say, the Westernizing of Oriental art? There is, by the bye, a politer synonym for the adjective just quoted—namely "natural." But I am not proposing that we should Westernize Oriental art, merely that we should modernize it,—a different thing. At Orientalized Western architecture the purist might justly look askance, not so at modernized Oriental architecture. That could be, and should be living art. Nor am I advocating "another futile revival" (one of the ill-names that have been used in the present controversy). The survival of the living tradition is sufficient guarantee against that. Futility in all art movements has been due to a lack of conviction on the part of the artists, a desire merely for novelty in default of inspiration. But where in the world could the architect, who had lived long enough with the art of India to become imbued with a sympathetic understanding of it, find a more inspiring task than the development of that art, and the bringing it up to date? Futility and banality and everything that means failure cannot, of course, be insured against with respect to any work or art movement. I say only that in this one there are fewer elements of danger and more of hope than in most.

Can a developed Indian architecture provide us with buildings that are modern, convenient, economical? I think so. Will they not rather be unpractical and over-ornate? I think not. All depends on the handling of the material, or rather on the architects who handle it. In spite of such individual examples as may be cited to support a contrary view, there is nothing really inherent in Indian art that demands over-elaboration or unpracticality and inconvenience, even in the light of the most diverse and exacting modern requirements. There is no element calling for lavish expenditure that is not fortuitous, or that is not as capable as corresponding elements in other modes of architectural expression of being overcome by skill on the part of the designer.

Then there is what has been called the "bogey of style" (another of the ill-names). We are told that we must not build in an Indian or any other definite manner because of this "bogey." Under this head there has been written a great deal calculated to bring hopeless confusion to the mind of the unhappy layman who has been trying to follow the discussion. He must have gathered that all style was an offence to the canons of art, that observance of conditions was the only guide, and he must have pictured the box or barn as the only types of legitimate design. He may have believed himself bidden to shudder at the enormity of a Government which has the temerity to say it wants its buildings in this style or in that. The fact is it is the most difficult thing in the world to write or speak clearly and unmistakeably about anything having to do with art. Art and artists are full of subtilties, and these don't make for definiteness. But I cannot refrain from one more attempt to make this difficult point clearer. The layman is wrong who thinks, and the artist is wrong who leads him to think that any cannon of art is controverted by the old proverb, "He who pays the piper has a right to call the tune." But it is a mistake to call a tune which any particular piper cannot or does not wish to play. That is why Government is belaboured for making Barry turn the Houses of Parliament into Gothic, and Scott the Home Office into Renaissance. Who pays the piper has also the responsibility (to ordinary business principles) of seeing he gets that piper who can best play the tune he wants. Style to the architect is like language to the speaker. It is a necessity of articulate expression. We do not wish to hear a man speak in any language with which he is not so familiar that he can think in it. So we do not wish an architect to work in a style into which his thoughts do not jump direct without the intervention of a more familiar medium from which he has to translate them. We don't want "broken" language. And of course we do not wish the architect to be a mere compiler of "elegant extracts." We have seen too much of that already.

The initiator of a building project, be he a private individual or a Government, has not only a right but a duty to indicate his wishes clearly on all points even including style, but he has not a right to coerce his architect or to impose on him conditions he is not both able and cordially willing to accept. To do so has always imperilled the success of the work and moreover has exposed the architect to the unfortunate imputation of venality. It has also been unfair to a profession that might have provided a man equally able and more in sympathy with the intentions of the initiator.

Therefore I cannot see, if we declare it to be our architectual policy to develop Indian art, that we shall be transgressing the canons either of art or of commonsense. To my mind we shall rather be transgressing both, if we do not.

Nothing else that we can do will better help to clear the way to the opening up of the profession of the architect to the youth of India, to whom it has hitherto seemed to have its doors closed. Not otherwise could we hope to see them bring to it that enthusiasm without which no art can flourish at all, and without which we could hardly hope that the Indian student would persevere through the drudgery of the learning of architecture. For while the architect has, like the poet, to be born, he has also to be made. The arduousness of this process of making is seldom realized by anyone but the architect. It does not mean the committing to memory of facts and figures, though that comes into it too. Men have to "go through the mill," to work hard and long, and thus to get their whole mental apparatus shaped, sharpened and tempered as in perhaps no other calling. And the trouble of it is there exist practically no "mills" in the country for the purpose. These are, I hope, being built up, but that will take time. So the architectural aspirant may have to endure exile as well as drudgery, and nothing but enthusiasm will bring him unscathed through that. When we have a sufficiency of Indian youths of the right stamp thoroughly grounded in the principles of architectural design as these are understood in Europe and America—but nowhere better than in the architectural schools of Britain—when we have these men applying their trained minds to designing for the complex problems of modern life in India, drawing their inspiration from the best examples of old work and traditional work in the country, we shall not have long to wait, comparatively speaking, before we see an indigenous profession firmly established, and an indigenous architecture at once modern and distinctively Indian, carrying on the traditions of art, and putting renewed life into the crafts of building.

Our declaration of architectural policy could take no more suitable form than that of the manner of design we adopt for New Delhi. Our forefathers of a hundred years ago sounded a certain note in the design of the earlier buildings of Calcutta, but that note has, I think it must be admitted, dwindled too often to a sorry squeak in later examples in the same city. Is it not arguable that this decadence was due to the keynote being out of tune with any indigenous tradition ? It was something of the nature of a revival, exotic, fortuitous, we introduced into India, and this, like others, has succumbed to the danger of revivals. Besides, it typed a period that is past—that of the mere Western occupation of the country. It would be a fitting thing if the architectural note we sound in our new Capital were to type the reawakened India of the present and future. In this matter practical and economical considerations seem to me to join hands with those which are artistic and sentimental. We have got our art—why waste it ? We have got our craftsmen—why employ them on work for which they have small aptitude—or (which is what would happen) leave our best craftsmen out altogether ? There is nothing, as I have already said, in an Indian manner of design that makes it costly, indeed my own experience goes to prove that the costliest manner for building in India is a Renaissance or classical one. Again, why should a Western manner be held to type most fittingly the spirit of the Government of India ? Why should the style of our Capital be such as to express most strongly those alien characteristics in the administration which every year tend more and more to disappear ? And lastly, why sound again a note that is sure to dwindle into decadence as it has done before, rather than one more likely to be worthily sustained by the future generations of indigenous architects for whose advent we might well make it our duty to prepare ?

Meanwhile, till we have a sufficiency of indigenous architects, there is no alternative but to be content with the substitute of European birth. It is not impossible for the European architect to work in the spirit of this country if he already finds himself in sympathy with it and is careful not to make the attempt on immature study. The great principles of art are the same the world over, through the medium of whatever "language" we express them. There are some of us who have made the attempt, and are still persisting in it, not, I think, without success ; and, had we received the support and encouragement that a fraction of such a wave of enthusiasm as the present would have afforded us, had we been made aware by the least hint that we were doing anything of which India as a people approved, we might have done more and better. For it is no confession of weakness to say that appreciation is as the breath of life to the artist ; appreciation and enthusiasm are the breath of life of art. If the project of New Delhi meant nothing else but to supply the stimulus for this popular enthusiasm for art it would not have come in vain. The really important thing, however, is that the nation should respond to the call. If India is really in earnest in her desire for an architecture of her own let her set about giving her sons to it.

J. BEGG, F.R.I.B.A.,

Consulting Architect to the Government of India.

Simla, December 1912.

FOREWORD.

THE following notes are the outcome of a suggestion made in a letter* from the India Society to the India Office, that, "in view of the importance of investigating the principles and practice of the living art and craft of India," the officers of the Archæological Department might be instructed to photograph, when on tour, interesting types of modern Indian buildings in the districts in which they are engaged, and to note on the craftsmen responsible for their design and decoration. They deal only with the local architecture of a small portion of northern India, and that but briefly.

My first step on receipt of instructions from my Government was to enquire from the officials (both of the Public Works and of the Revenue and Agriculture Departments) in the various divisions of the Punjab and United Provinces, as to whether they knew of any buildings of the types instanced in the letter of the India Society, so that I might see and photograph them on my next visit. In response to my enquiries twenty-nine replies were received to the effect that there were no such buildings, while seven replies referred me to examples at Agra, Delhi, Lucknow, Allahabad, Muttra, Amritsar and Saharanpur.

My own circle did not yield much, and it was during a special visit to the Native States of Rajputana, primarily for the purpose of collecting antiquities for the Historical and Archæological Loan Exhibition held at Delhi during the Darbar period and cold season of 1911-12, that this information was principally collected. It need hardly be said that it is scanty; for my regular work this year has been exceptionally heavy owing to the Darbar, and I have not, therefore, been able to give as much time to the project as I could have wished. In truth, a subject of this kind needs handling on a far larger scale than has been possible here; so much so, that it would have been preferable, perhaps, to collect further information from other localities on the matter before any publication was issued. In view, however, of the importance attaching to indigenous architecture in connection with the building of the new Capital of Delhi, which has been decided on since the India Society despatched their letter under reference, the Government of India have instructed me to prepare this report without delay.

Let me add that it has been extremely difficult to ascertain any of the names of the craftsmen engaged on the work of these buildings. They are of the humblest class, and several officials, who showed me over these modern buildings, ridiculed the idea of asking for their names and addresses; indeed, several of the men themselves, when asked, looked on me with suspicion and, thinking that I might be on some other quest, gave me wrong addresses. Nor was a short stay of a day or two in each place sufficient time in which to get together much information. However, if the men are wanted, they can readily be found.

---

* Dated the 20th November 1910, and reprinted, together with the correspondence on the subject between the Imperial and Local Government in the appendix to this report.

DELHI.

The *dharmsala* of Chunna Mall (Plate 2), in the *Mohalla Nil ka Katra,* has just been completed. It was built under the supervision of Nuru, *mistri,* who did not receive any regular pay but charged commission, *dasturi,* on all the materials purchased for the building. His commission, according to the owner, amounted to about Rs. 20 or Rs. 25 per month. In return, he spent a few hours daily at the building, gave instructions to the masons for the next day's work, and paid them. Such *mistris* at Delhi usually have several works going on at once. They make rough plans showing the arrangements of the rooms, and, for important buildings, sometimes prepare a front elevation. I am indebted for this information to Rai Bahadur Bishambar Nath, Executive Engineer of Gurgaon. He also says that, as far as he knows, they never prepare any sections showing inner details of roof beams and *ballis.* Details of decoration are very seldom made except for teaching novices. It will be seen from this how much is left to the mason, on 8 to 10 annas per day.

The *dharmsala* has a Gothic feeling about its lower door and window openings, perhaps suggested by the Gothic work of the Mutiny memorial on the Ridge at Delhi, and the band of carved foliage which frames the entrance is a fine piece of work. The Gothic touch is not so fortunate in the *chattris* of this building. They look too spidery, but, in spite of the blemishes, one cannot help feeling that there has been a "thinking" mind behind the whole design and a praiseworthy endeavour to evolve some new expression.

The same remarks apply to the *dharmsala* of Lachmi Narain (Plate 3), near the Fathpuri Masjid, but, as in the first, the upper storey rather spoils the rest. It looks as if money had run short, and as if they had been obliged to finish in cast and corrugated iron what was originally intended to be in stone.

AGRA.

Pietra Dura.—The important part that this industry plays in the decoration of Indian architecture is well known.

The following notes were taken at the workshops of Nathoo Ram at Agra, whose ancestors for several generations had carried on the same industry, and who expressed regret that his son was taking up the medical profession. There is a marked absence of European influence in the work of this firm. Old pattern-books, filled with measured drawings of the best examples of Mughal work, form the basis of their designs. It is true that there is no seeking after new designs, and mere mechanical copying without doubt tends to deterioration of the original, but it is better at any rate that there should be no adaptation of extraneous forms, the *motif* of which might not be understood, and which without artistic education would be bound to be a failure. The stages through which a finished piece of *pietra dura* work passes are these :—(Plate 4).

Stage 1.—The stones for inlay are given first to the cutter, *katai,* who cuts the stone into thin "wafers," about 1/16th of an inch in thickness. This he does by means of a bow saw, *kamani*, the saw being a piece of iron wire stretched taut on a bow.

The stone he has to cut is held in a peg, *thya*, in the top of which is a groove in which the stone is fixed and held tight with lac. The *thya* is held in a block of stone. By his side is a bowl of water, a bowl of moist emery powder, which he uses to quicken the action of the saw, and also a box of stones to be cut into "wafers," these last being given out as required by the head of the firm. The wages of the *katai* are Rs. 10 per mensem.

Stage 2.—The "wafers," when ready, are handed to the "trimmer," who puts an even surface on them, and removes the minutest irregularities left on them by the *kamani*. This he does by rubbing the surface on a polishing wheel or *ghisiya*, made of emery and lac, and revolved by means of a bow string. In the photograph the "trimmer" may be seen holding the stone against the side of the *ghisiya*. He then rubs the "wafer" approximately into the shape required, a flower petal, a leaf, or the like, and, on its completion, it is stuck on a piece of glass by means of clay and placed beside the man who is engaged on the actual work of inlaying. These may be seen ready for use on the table top shown in Plate 5. The trimmer is usually an apprentice. He gets no pay, but hopes eventually to become a *puchhekar*, the man who does the actual inlaying work.

Stage 3.—The *puchhekar* has already transferred the pattern from the drawing to the surface to be inlaid. This is done by tracing the pattern on to a mica sheet, the outlines of the designs being then pricked through on to the surface to be inlaid. He cuts holes of the required shape in the surface to be inlaid with small chisels, *tanki*, of which there are two varieties. The sharp-pointed kind is called *narga*, and the chisel-edged kind *nargi*. The latter vary in width at the cutting end, but their length is generally the same, 8 inches. A heap of them is seen lying at his side. He has also another instrument, *saun* (made of emery and lac), on which he sharpens his chisels, or trims up, if necessary, the stone to be fitted into the hole.

The stones are fixed in with a native cement, *masala*, composed of white lead, resin and wax. A piece of glass is then laid over the surface, and on it is placed a piece of burning charcoal so as to anneal the inlay. In larger works the pieces are put in with best quality lime.

Plate 5 shows the drawing from which an inlaid chess table is being made. All the different colours of the stones to be used are indicated on the drawing, which is prepared by the head of the firm.

The *puchhekar* gets Rs. 20 a month. In Plate 5 two *puchhekars* are seen at work.

Stage 4.—After the whole surface is "inlaid," it is handed to the *polisher*. There are three processes in polishing—

(*a*) The surface is first rubbed with emery and lac, into which a little water has been mixed.

(*b*) It is then rubbed with fine dust, which has fallen from the stones when being trimmed into shape by the *ghisiya*.

(*c*) Finally it is polished with putty powder or acetate of lead.

All the workmen engaged here are natives of Agra. The *puchhekars* have been many years with the firm and were first trained as apprentices. Considering the work they execute, Rs. 20 per month is but a small wage.

Some of the stones used in inlay are—

Lapis Lazuli	... *Lajward.*	From Afghanistan and Ceylon.	
Cornelian	... *Akik.*	„	Ratanpur.
Bloodstone	... *Pitonia*	„	Jubbulpur.
Plum-pudding stone	... *Godaria.*		
Yellow marble	... *Khattu.*	„	Jeysalmir.
Conchshell	... *Sankh.*		
Onyx ...	... *Sang-i-Sulamani.*	Jubbulpur, and Ratanpur, Rajpipla.	
Agate ...	... *Akik.* (1)	„	„
Jasper ...	... *Akik.*	„	„
Amethyst...	... *Jamunia.*		
Cairngorm	... *Dhundela.*		
Moss-agate	... *Shajar.*		
Sand ...	... *Kirkira.*		

Black marble is practically unknown in India, although a dark variety is found at Bhainslana in Rajputana.

Working in soapstone (kharia) (Plate 6). This is done by the same firm. The stone comes from Karauli State and costs Rs. 3 per *maund.* The workman in the photo. gets Rs. 15 a month, and designed the tray himself. Workmen of this kind should readily take to modern decorative plaster work.

Jali work. Plate 7.—Men are shown here at work on a *jali* screen. Hardly any Indian building is without a piece of this pierced stone work. The design illustrated, which is perhaps not a very good one, is drawn out by a draftsman (Rs. 20 per mensem) on the stone. The masons (8 to 10 annas per diem) carve it out. As a rule, the latter draw it out themselves, without any help from a draftsman. Two drawings from one of Nathoo Ram's pattern-books are shown in Plate 8.

The Daoji Temple at Agra. Plate 10.—This is one of the most interesting buildings I have seen. So far, it has been nearly 10 years in building, and, at the rate it is going on, will be as many more before it is finished. I was told that it had cost over Rs. 20,000 so far, but cannot vouch for these figures. There is no architect, no plan, and no programme of work.

The man on the left in the photograph, Plate 9, is named Kalyan, of Namnir, Agra. He has worked on the building from the start and is now head *mistri,* the original head *mistri* being dead. Both these men are true master craftsmen. They receive 10 annas per day and do all the work. One or two coolies are brought in to help in getting the larger stones into position. The entrance to the temple on the road side gives but little idea of the size of the courtyard behind, which is divided into a lower and upper portion, the latter leading to the inner shrine of the temple. Above are living rooms. The building is late Mughal in feeling, but on to it has been grafted the Bharatpur style of carving, the result, no doubt, of the numerous inroads made by that State into Agra during the later days of the Mughal empire. The carving lacks beauty in

(1) Agate is called *gawa* at Jubbulpur.

expression, the figures are poor, and the dwarf columns are without character. Above them, too, has been introduced a circular arch. The true constructional spirit of architecture may, however, be seen in the pilasters on the wall behind these dwarf columns. But, as an example of architecture by men untutored in its practice and relying solely on their traditional knowledge, this little building is worthy of close attention.

Masons at present in the United Provinces are, I am informed, of only one or two years' standing. They start by working as ordinary coolies, their ambition being eventually to become contractors. Their wages are 8 to 10 annas per day. Plastering for ordinary work is done by coolies at 6 to 8 annas per day, while for better work there are special plasterers, who get 8 to 10 annas. I am not, of course, referring to Public Works Department prices, although I believe these are about the same.

Another most interesting new building at Agra is the *samadh* for Swamiji Maharaj, now being built about a mile beyond the Roman Catholic Cemetery, Civil Lines (Plates 11 and 12). The architect is Babu Tota Ram. This ambitious structure was begun in May 1904, and so far has not reached the first floor level. The work is being carried on very slowly by daily labour, and it is estimated that the building will cost 25 lakhs to complete. The design shows a blending of Gothic and Saracenic. The quality of the masonry work is excellent. The building is to be of brick, faced with marble, and its total height when finished is intended to top the Taj Mahal. The dome and its finials, are, unfortunately, out of proportion with the substructure, and it is doubtful if their immense weight could be safely sustained. Still, the design shows some ingenuity. A suggestion for the modified treatment of one of the four corner *chattris*, is seen in Plate 13.

Some huge girders are seen in front of the building. I could not quite make out whether they were either too heavy for the masonry or too light for the weight they had to carry, but it seems they cannot be used, although acquired at a great cost, and will have to be sold for what they can fetch, which is not likely to be much.

The money for the building is being collected only very gradually, and it will take many years to complete.

ALLAHABAD.

Two modern houses at Allahabad, owned by Lala Bisheshar Das and Lala Misri Lal, are shown in Plates 14 and 15. The latter owner says in a letter :—" both our buildings were constructed without any professional help. The plan of the building (*sic*) is that of my brother, who also supervised the construction. He is an amateur architect."

LUCKNOW.

The Nudwat-ul-ulama, (Plates 16 and 17), an Indian Collegiate building now under construction at Lucknow, is interesting as illustrating the continuance of the style of architecture peculiar to Lucknow. The main entrance to the building is after the style of the Rumi Darwaza, while the arches of the verandah bear a strong resemblance to those seen in the buildings erected in the days of the Sovereigns of Oudh.

A large domed hall, 73′ 0″ × 40′ 0′, will be the chief feature of the building, which is surrounded on all sides by a verandah. The building is single storeyed with the exception of the hall and the four octagonal towers at each corner.

Up to date the building has cost Rs. 65,000, of which Rs. 50,000 were given by Her Highness, the Begam of Bhawalpur. The designs were furnished by Khan Bahadur Saiyid Jafar Husain, Manager, Tanks Division, Jhansi, while the construction work is under the supervision of Munshi Muhammad Ehteshan Ali, who is also the Building Secretary of the Institution.

AJMER.

The modern local architecture here is especially interesting, as it shows signs of being already affected by European influence. Ajmer has been in British territory since 1818. The house in Plate 18 was built by a native mason. There is a general lack of character about the façade, and it is meagre in detail. The round arch forms are not happy. The house in Plate 19 is also poor. The *chajja* does not return round the side of the building, and the little projecting balconies at either side of the entrance look as if they had been stuck on.

Plate 20 is the only one of the Ajmer buildings illustrated here which has been designed by a draftsman, Ganga Din by name. The general lines are good, but the building would have been better without the painting. He has probably been influenced in his design by the house in Plate 21, about which there is something very pleasing. The blank wall of its lower storey is in sharp contrast with the richness of the first floor. The string course, running to the end of the range of buildings, ties them together admirably, while the continuity of effect, produced by the *chajjas* and their deep shadows, is good. The paintings on the wall at either side of the gate give a splash of colour and realism to the façade. This house, rather older than the others, was built by a native mason.

The gateway of the Arya Samaj Press, Plate 22, also the work of native masons, has something solid and sensible about it, but there is a not quite happy air about the brackets supporting the balcony at the first floor level, the projections of which at either end are too slight to be of any value.

The marble *chattri* in Saraoji's garden (Plate 23) is reminiscent of late Mughal work. It was built by a native mason.

Ajmer masons receive from 8 to 10 annas per day and *mistris* about Rs. 20 per month.

BHOPAL.

The Taj-ul-Masajid, now building, will be, I think, the largest modern mosque in India. It was begun during the time of the late Begam of Bhopal. The plan and elevation, Plate 24, were prepared by Muhammad Raushan, a Delhi draftsman, now dead, but all details are being worked out, as the work goes on, by the contractors. At present two contractors are at work on the mosque, the south gate and arcades being done by one Rathaji from Kach near Kathiawar. The east gate is the work of another contractor. I saw workmen laying the stone floor of the arcades. They were getting 8 to 10 annas per day and I was told they worked out all masonry details. Plate 27 shows the east gate in course of construction.

The lowest steps have already been set, and the great elevation of the mosque courtyard above the road level can easily be judged. A curious feature is the *Zanana* gallery seen in Plates 25 and 28. In the latter, the drum of the north dome can be seen rising above the cresting of the roof. The *minars* are to be 170′ 6″ in height when finished, and the State Engineer told me he hoped to use reinforced concrete in their construction. The mosque measures 261′ 6″ North and South by 88′ 0″ East and West. Its treatment is distinctly new. At either end are commodious *Zanana* chapels, while the *Zanana* gallery and the mezzanine floor at each end of the mosque, near the minars, are also novel features. There is a boldness of treatment about the *chattri* in Plate 30. Her Highness the Begam frequently visits the work and gives orders as to details, and it is hoped that the building, which is an eloquent testimony to the fact that the old Indian builders have not lost their skill, will be finished ere long.

Another new mosque is that of Kulsum Bi. It was begun in 1898, took four years to build, and cost Rs. 30,000. It was designed by Muhammad Taqi and Hur Lal, part of the work being done by contract through the first named, and the rest by daily labour through Hur Lal. The entrance (Plate 31) is rather weak in design, and it is feared that some of its details have been inspired by those of the old palace buildings (Plate 32). These show the unintelligent use of European forms, which is the characteristic of the buildings erected in Lucknow at the end of the 18th century by the Sovereigns of Oudh. It was, however, erected some time ago, and there is no sign of anything similar among the new buildings of Bhopal.

A typical Bhopal town house is illustrated in the frontispiece. All walls in Bhopal are provided with *chajjas* at frequent intervals, to shade them and to throw off the rain.

There is good local building stone in Bhopal, prices for paving being Rs. 50 per 150 sq. ft., while prices for masonry work range from Rs. 15 to Rs. 35 per 100 cub. ft., according to the quality required. Masons and carpenters receive 8 to 10 annas per day. Here, as at Bikanir, local building is largely encouraged by the present ruler.

BIKANIR.

The area of the city, which is crowded with excellent specimens of modern architecture of a most characteristic type, is broken up into a series of little open squares, round which the houses are built. Among the citizens of Bikanir there seems to be some real rivalry in the matter of their houses, the very best stimulant that can be given to architecture. Many of them are of the wealthy *bania* caste, and their dwellings, besides being externally of considerable pretensions, are fitted within with electric light, electric fans, and other appurtenances of modern comfort.

All the buildings illustrated here, unless otherwise stated, are the work of master masons, natives of Bikanir, working at the rate of annas 8 to Re. 1 daily. To quote the Assistant State Engineer of Bikanir, who kindly accompanied me on my inspection, "they don't believe in plans." Their names and addresses I was not able to ascertain, as I was only in Bikanir 48 hours, but it is sufficient to say that they can be found at any time when required. The exterior of Moti Mal's house (Plates 33 and 34) seems to indicate clearly the purpose for which the interior is to be used. The large barred doorways suggest a private courtyard, the traceried windows and balconies of the upper floors the ladies' apartments, and the roof, crowned with a balustrade, a place where the evening breezes may be enjoyed. The owner is seen standing at what might be termed the "stoep" of his house, a sort of subsidiary entrance flanked by open verandahs, where he can see his friends or hold converse with passers-by, the larger gateway being only used for weddings or other important family gatherings. The curved *chajjas* are interesting and illustrate their "bamboo" prototype [1]; curious too are the little pendants hanging from the outer edges of the balconies, giving them an air of lightness and delicacy.

There is something very dignified in the façade in Plate 35, and it owes its stately and imposing character largely to the multiplication of horizontal bands and lines which combine with the perpendicular in a manner suggestive of Chalukyan architecture. Symmetry is marked. The doorways are emphasised by the projecting bays above them, while the mason has still further endeavoured to accentuate the central bay by the addition of some extra carving on the crowning balustrade. There is a predilection for minute and profuse ornament, an evident indifference to cost and labour, those peculiarities in Indian architecture which are so hard to explain. Sandstone is procured near Bikanir, a grey and red variety being obtained from the same quarry. Ordinary face work set in position costs 13½ annas per cubic foot, while better quality work costs one rupee. Carving is paid for according to the quality of the work, panels and string courses per square foot and columns per cubic foot. I was told that private people get the work much cheaper than the State, as is the case in British India. Plate 36 shows Mehta Street, at the end of which is a house no whit inferior in design. Its upper storeys are, if anything, more elaborately carved.

Other examples are seen in Plates 37 and 38. The former has a more European feeling about the carving of the upper storey, and there is the suggestion of an entablature above the columns of the verandah. Panna Lall's Mandir is, unlike the other houses which are all of red

---

[1] Fergusson. *History of Indian and Eastern Architecture.* Vol II, page 159.

"The exceptional style is that which grew up in Bengal proper and is practised generally in the province at the present day. It may have existed from an early date, but no very old examples are known, and it is consequently impossible to feel sure about this. Its leading characteristic is the bent cornice, copied from the bamboo huts of the natives. To understand this, it may be as well to explain that the roof of the huts in Bengal are formed of two rectangular frames of bamboos, perfectly flat and rectangular when formed, but when lifted from the ground and fitted to the substructure they are bent so that the elasticity of the bamboo, resisting the flexure, keeps all the fastenings in a state of tension, which makes a singularly firm roof out of very frail materials. It is the only instance I know of elasticity being employed in building, but is so singularly successful in attaining the desired end, and is so common, that we can hardly wonder when the Bengalis turned their attention to more permanent modes of building they should have copied this one."

sandstone, built of marble. There is something dignified about the lower verandah, and one cannot help feeling what a fine effect could be obtained if these houses were side by side in one street. As it is, they but too often stand alone with dwellings of the meanest kind on either side of them. I noticed that in the rubble masonry walls of these latter there were courses of brick laid herring-bone fashion, every 6 feet. This is, I suppose, to tie the walls together and to distribute the weight evenly and at intervals on the inferior rubble walling.

Plate 39 is another house similar in character to the one shown in Plate 33. The simplicity of its lower portion is in marked contrast to the work of the upper storeys. In front of the house can be seen the table or *takht*, on which the resident of Bikanir sits daily between 4 and 5 p.m. The time between 12 and 4 p.m. is spent by the master of the house in his own apartments, while after 5 p.m. he goes to join the ladies and to take his food.

An interior is seen in Plate 40. Many will no doubt be hard on it and with reason. Its decoration is not good and the fanlights and curved door-heads are out of keeping with the purely Indian exterior of this house. However, these are excrescences, which a little artistic education would remove. One must not forget the hideous wall papers, the night-mare gas brackets, and the ugly doors and windows which are still to be found in many an English home, and one must remember how recently our own taste has demanded simplicity and restfulness. The main essentials of the room are correct enough. Its many doors and windows high up in the wall make it cool, while the little gallery is a pleasing feature. By substituting doors and windows of Indian pattern and by eliminating the painted decoration, the appearance of the room would be made a pleasant one, and with *pardahs* of some local fabric instead of the imported chintz, the change would be complete. The chintz curtains in this room illustrate the attitude of the Indian towards European art. He has not been educated to it and does not know what to take and what to reject. The falling off in the interior of this house as compared with the exterior is curious, and one wonders if it is due to some desire on the part of the owner (who will, I hope, forgive me for thus endeavouring to analyse his thoughts) to conform to European ideas, while he does not wish to appear publicly to imitate them, and so builds the outside of his house in his own traditional style. Let no one condemn the electric fans and lighting as being out of keeping with the house. It is well known how much they contribute to comfort in India, and those who can afford to have them are to be envied.

Plate 41 shows the new entrance façade to the Durga Mandir. It is like the domestic work, but the idea of the building having a higher function is shown by the *chattri* on the roof, which perhaps rises rather too abruptly from the substructure. Plate 42 shows two new marble mausolea at Devi Kund, the burying place of the rulers of Bikanir. The way in which their builders have carried on the traditional idea of the columns in the panelling below them is worthy of notice.

The floor of the temple of Saida Sukh in Plate 43 is laid with a pleasing design in black and white marble. The temple took about two years to build and cost Rs. 80,000.

Plate 44 shows the new façade for Rati Bihari's temple, now being built by local contract according to His Highness the Maharajah's own ideas, and which bids fair when finished to keep up the reputation of Bikanir architecture. The work will cost about a lakh.

The new teak wood door in the Old Palace, shown in Plate 45, was executed by boys of not more than 15 years of age, and in the plate below it the carpenters (8 to 10 annas per diem) are seen preparing another like it. The fine old door (Plate 47) at the house of Sri Krishan Dass has no doubt served to imbue many a present day Bikanir craftsman with the traditional spirit, as has the silver door in Plate 48, which is also older work. The handles are rings held in the trunk of an elephant which is carrying a *mahout*.

This capacity for building-craft, so evidently possessed by the inhabitants of Bikanir, has been without doubt encouraged by the presence in their midst of the old palace, the façade of which is seen in Plate 49. It is no longer used as a permanent residence by H. H. the Maharajah, a new palace, Lalgarh, having been built some little distance from the city. The old palace is a most imposing structure. The long line of pierced stone screens with the pillared verandah above them, gives an appearance of lightness to the mass. The architect has, with curious inconsistency, carried this verandah through the half octagon projections crowned by cupolas, thereby rather taking away their sense of strength. As in many Indian buildings, one looks vainly at first for the entrance, for it is tucked away in an obscure corner, and does not strike the European eye as being sufficiently imposing for its function. Within the palace are labyrinths of rooms, each vying with the other in its scheme of decoration. (Plates 50 and 51.) Reached by dark and narrow corridors, dimly lit yet glittering with glass and gold, they breathe of the intrigue and luxury so dear to the Oriental mind.

Painted decoration, such as is seen in Plate 51, costs Re. 1 per square foot.

Plate 52 shows the main courtyard of the palace now undergoing repairs. The building to the right, erected by one of Bikanir's former rulers, shows the Indian *chajja*, combined with an European treatment of column and entablature, and the result is not unhappy, jumble of styles though it is.

The new Darbar hall in the old palace at Bikanir was begun in 1887 and completed in 1896. It was worked out by local craftsmen and is a fine piece of work, built at the express wish of H. H. the Maharajah in the local style. Raising its head proudly over the city which encircles it, it must appeal strongly to the sentiment of the inhabitants as being the place wherein their rulers hold audience. (Plate 53.)

Plate 54 shows the courtyard of this new Darbar hall, with the ladies' gallery above. There is originality in every line of it down to the smallest detail. The design of the almost Corinthian capitals, the three centred arches, and the carving which adorns them, has all been carefully thought out. The south-east corner of the hall, the photo. of which is taken from the 'approach terrace,' is a splendid piece of work. (Plate 55.) There is an air of delightful incongruousness about it. A spherical bay window, supported by a half column and set in an angle of the building rests "cheek by jowl" with two other projecting windows. The imagination of the builder has had full play. The contractor was one Bokar of Jodhpur, which perhaps accounts for the similarity between the work on this portion of the hall and the old palace in the Fort at Jodhpur.

H. H. the Maharajah's new palace at Lalgarh was designed by Sir Swinton Jacob, but all the details were worked out by native craftsmen. His Highness took a personal interest in the work and great credit is undoubtedly due to him for the suggestions which he made from time to time to suit his requirements or his ideas, and for the pleasing and useful additions which resulted from them.

H. H. the Maharajah has done much to encourage the crafts of his subjects during recent years. His new palace is, like the interior of the new Darbar hall (Plates 56, 57 and 58), covered with a profusion of carving, while the ground in front of the Fort is now being laid out on monumental lines at the cost of 4 lakhs raised by public subscription with a grant-in-aid from the State.

The following are the names of the principal local craftsmen in Bikanir who can build houses of the type illustrated herein:—Gulama, Budhan, Mua, Shivbux, Narain, Bhikka, Avaru, Nathu, Khudabux, Rupa, Prabhu, Girdhari, Anna, Amru, (1) Mukua, (2) Mukua, Khian, Indrabhan, Dewa, (1) Ramchand, (2) Ramchand, Gordhan, Lichman, Fakira, Bulakhi.

GWALIOR.

The chief features of the houses at Gwalior are the lace-like stone screens of the upper storeys. They are generally whitewashed and in the strong sunlight this rather adds to their effect. Plates 59 and 60 are examples of typical Gwalior houses. They are executed and designed by the local native masons paid at the rate of 8 to 10 annas daily.

Plate 61 shows a little projecting balcony over the entrance to a temple, and Plate 62, Girdhari Mal's house. It is an effective treatment for the corner of a street, although the corrugated iron erection on the top storey might be advantageously dispensed with. Plate 63 shows the type of arcading found along many of the principal thoroughfares. It is a pity that European details have crept into its design, as the general idea of small houses with shops below is a good one. The new Hindu temple (Plate 64) built by Prince Bhaiya Balwant Rao, an Indian architect, is a happy combination of the Hindu and Mughal styles. The carving, Plate 65, with which it is covered, is perhaps rather too rich for European ideas, but is of undoubted ability. The interior, with its black and white marble floor, is most imposing, and the carving has been used here with more restraint than on the outside, thereby producing an effect of solidity and strength (Plate 66). The excellent Hindu architecture of the Fort at Gwalior, which served as a model to the Mughals when designing similar edifices, is no doubt to a great extent responsible for the ability of the present Gwalior builders.

The only Indian architect in the state is Prince Bhaiya Balwant Rao. He recently designed the theatre and market buildings. Jugal Kishore, who has worked for 15 years under Prince Bhaiya Balwant Rao, was closely connected with the work on the above buildings and has opened an office in the city where designs are prepared and works supervised.

The following craftsmen in the State are well up in building houses in the native style and in executing carved ornamental work. Their usual wages are 10 to 12 annas per day, but, if working out of Gwalior, they receive double these amounts.

Har Pershad, Mansa Ram, Ganesh, Nainsuk, Dhani Ram, Badri, Dhanno Ram, Gajjoo, Lalloo Ram—residents of old Gwalior city, and Kishen Dass, Amar Singh, Ram Dayal, Lalji, Jagannath, Har Pershad, Thakur Dass, Nanna, Tika Ram—residents of Lashkar.

JAIPUR.

There is no doubt that the natives of Jaipur take naturally to all kinds of design. The work done by the School of Art is well known, while there are many other craftsmen in the city who can turn out work of equal quality. The large number of buildings recently erected by the State and by Sir Swinton Jacob has no doubt nurtured the inborn keenness of the men of Jaipur for the several crafts. Some of the works of Lala Chiman Lall, the State architect, are illustrated. Other able Indians in the State are Lala Shankar Lall, who was trained in Jaipur and has never left it. He gained the second place in the competition for the Prince of Wales' memorial in Bombay, and first prize in the competition for the new courts at Hyderabad in the Deccan. I am told by Sir Swinton Jacob that he has not been trained as 'an architect in the highest sense,' but that he has brains and knows how to use them. Lately, he has been endeavouring to obtain some designation better than "Head Draftsman," and this he undoubtedly deserves.

Lal Chand, in the Superintending Engineer's Office, is another clever and capable man, and these two have helped to train competent draftsmen, several of whom have found good places elsewhere.

The European architect is apt to be too hard on the Indian members of the profession. It is, perhaps, largely due to the fact that he does not appreciate the fact that native life in Native States has not appreciably changed since Mughal days. There is consequently no marked change in the architecture, which is the expression of that life. The buildings illustrated here reflect this spirit of conservatism. They are suited to their requirements in every respect, and as such are embodiments of living art, with every right to a place in the history of architecture. The men who have been responsible for them possess faculties not only for construction but for design also, as well as a working knowledge of allied crafts such as carpentry and metal work. But their only school as yet is antiquity. Some of the illustrations show only too plainly the results of experiment in design without the requisite basis of education.

That the quality of the work of an Indian architect, when he embarks on a scheme involving other than purely native requirements, is not up to the standard of Europe, is owing to the fact that his knowledge of tradition is not backed up by a careful study of architectural history, design, and the use of modern methods of construction.

The guest house in the Jaipur palace (Plates 67 and 68) was designed by Lala Chiman Lall and carried out by daily labour. The ornament was sketched for the stone-cutters (8 annas per day) direct on the stone by draftsmen. The doors of this building are bound with brass. Carpenters get 6 to 7 annas and brass workers 8 annas per day. In the 'Sarad ki deori,' which can be seen on the extreme left of the photograph, the doors of brass alone cost Rs. 12,000, brass workers on the above wage being employed. It is said that many craftsmen and masons have left the State during the last 20 years owing to the increased demand for them in British India.

The grey sandstone used in Jaipur comes from Hindon, 100 miles away, and the marble from Raewala. Marble columns are cut, according to design, for Rs. 5 to Rs. 7 per cubic foot, the smaller the quantity the greater the price per cubic foot. Ordinary building stone, which is found in large quantities in the neighbouring hills, costs ready dressed Rs. 2 per cubic foot, and Rs. 50 per 1,000 cubic feet in the rough. No bricks are used. Some two to three lakhs are spent annually by the State on new buildings.

Plates 69, 70 and 71 show a royal mausoleum for the present ruler's wife. This is also the work of Lala Chiman Lall. Plate 72 illustrates some clay models for the mausoleum details, while the clay model of a parapet is being erected on the little *chattri* shown in Plate 73, so that its merits may be judged at the level at which it will be seen when finished. These models show the careful consideration that is being given to details.

Darogaji's house (Plate 74) is almost reminiscent of Florence. The high plinth reached by a sloping ramp is worthy of remark. The balcony and the *chajja* above it, respectively, mark the levels of the 1st and 2nd floors. The windows fronting on the street are small, light being obtained for the rooms from larger windows facing on the inner courtyard. Indeed, it appears as if the house was constructed from the point of view of defence. A narrow passage with several turns leads off the entrance porch to the interior of the house. The pictures at either side of the door give a pleasing touch of colour to the façade. The view of the interior courtyard (Plate 75) shows the *jali* screens that allow the ladies of the household to pass unobserved from room to room.

Isha Rana's house (Plate 76) in the Gopalji ka rasta, was designed and built entirely by native masons. It cost Rs. 30,000. The illustration shows the upper portion of the interior courtyard. Its extreme simplicity makes it attractive.

Plates 77 and 78 show typical Jaipur street architecture. It is almost invariably colourwashed pink and outlined in white, the effect produced being by no means a bad one. Plate 79 shows the interior of a house where an experiment has been made to adopt European forms without success.

JODHPUR.

Some apology must be made for including in this report some ancient buildings of Jodhpur Fort, but the influence they must have had, and are still having, on the traditional architecture of Rajputana, warrants their mention. Through the courtesy of the Jodhpur Darbar I was enabled to get these photographs of the interior of the Fort (Plates 80, 81, 82, 83, 84), which I cannot remember having seen hitherto published. For grandeur in conception and beauty of detail it is unsurpassed. Brackets, cornices and stone screens have been elaborated to the most picturesque richness.

The old palace of Maharaj Sur Singh also shows what the old Jodhpur builders could do (Plate 85). The Ransurji ka Mandir (Plate 86) was designed by Munshi Sub Lall, late of the Public Works Department, white marble and red sandstone being used in happy contrast. He is now practising as a local architect.

The next plate shows the shops at the opposite side of the street, which have been built by local masons. The temple of Raj Gopal (Plate 88) is another new building constructed locally. The new Government courts (Plate 89) were designed by Sir Swinton Jacob, but the execution of the ornament and carving was left entirely to the local masons. The latter get 10 to 12 annas per day. Rough sandstone costs Rs. 5 per cubic foot, and Rs. 15 ready dressed. The prices of Susegar sandstone, a harder variety, are 20 per cent. higher. No bricks are used in Jodhpur. A new market and clock tower are now being built from the designs of the State Engineer, at the cost of Rs. 1,60,000. The contractor is a local man, Kalla by name, and his work is excellent.

A special craft in Jodhpur is the inlaying of ebony with ivory. Ivory costs Rs. 14 per seer; its powder from sawing being used, I was told, as a tonic for buffaloes, so that there is no waste. A man I saw engaged on this work was getting Rs. 15 per month. He designed the pattern for inlay himself. I also saw at the same place, the Museum, a native artist working in oils. He was painting a picture of the late Maharajah from a photograph, on a wage of Rs. 20 per month.

The following masons and wood-workers can build a native house and execute its carved ornamental work:—Mustafa Khan, Abdul Rahman, Abdul Ghani, Azim-ud-din, Bhagwan Mali; the carpenters are Khian, Ram Ratan and Chuni Lal. The above receive from one to two rupees per day when engaged on such work in Jodhpur.

UDAIPUR.

My time here was short and almost entirely taken up with my archæological work; so my notes are few. A new Darbar hall, to cost 4 lakhs, is now being built by His Highness the Maharana, and will be well worth a visit when complete. It is done by daily labour which, I was told, His Highness prefers to contract work. The local masons are working out details of design and construction from plans prepared by the State.

Plate 90 shows a typical Udaipur house with shop below, and Plates 91, 92 are specimens of gateways. Plate 93 shows a street and characteristic arcading.

The following are the Indian architects in the State :—Jewan Ram Modi Ram, Amba Ram, Ganga Ram, Moti Lal, Bholi Ram, Nand Ram Nathu. The principal craftsmen are :—Balu and Gordhan, carpenters ; Nandu, Hira Lal and Jagannath, blacksmiths ; Liladhar, Kundan Lal and Panna Lal, decorative artists. The wages of these latter, if employed in Udaipur, run from ten annas to two rupees per day ; if they are employed outside the city, they receive higher rates.

SUMMARY.

There is no doubt that in British India the traditions of design and craftsmanship are in a stage of transition, as the photographs will clearly show, and this is largely due to—I quote the India Society's letter—"the spread of European fashion among the English educated classes in India and to departmental procedure in placing a very high premium upon the work of designers and craftsmen who merely imitate the commercial art of Europe." But I venture to think that there is another and perhaps more potent element in the decadence of the architecture of Northern India. A decline in Muhammadan architecture had set in as far back as the last years of Shah Jahan's reign, and before any very considerable European influence had been brought to bear on it. The mighty empire founded by Akbar was then already tottering to its fall. The Mughals, far from the invigorating surroundings of their native country, became feeble and luxurious. Their power was sapped by internal disorders, and without any extraneous influence there set in a spontaneous decline in their architecture from which it has never recovered. Its last real effort is seen in the elegance of the architecture of Shah Jahan, which had already lost the virility and originality of Akbar's buildings.

But the truth of the quotation from the Indian Society's letter is only too well borne out by some of the buildings which are here instanced. Every one who has been in India knows the unhappy erections that are so frequently met with in the "average Cantonment Station." Let us not be too hard on those who built them ; for until lately they have seen, springing up in their midst, buildings of the most mediocre architectural quality, and, at the worst, they have been striving after an ideal and endeavouring to express in their buildings the results of European influence. As a general rule too, they have had no training, and are of the humblest class. Small wonder, then, that their own output has likewise suffered. Improvement, however, in the taste of those whose ancestors showed themselves capable of such advanced artistic development, is sure to come with education established on the right lines.

In Rajputana, Indian life is very much the same as it was three or four centuries ago, and architecture is still a living art. In spite of the railways, telegraphs, and the visits their rulers and nobles pay so often to Western lands, it is almost purely *native*, and the building traditions are still unbroken. The buildings of Bikanir, for example, as surely represent the life and character of their occupants as do the low, small windowed and sturdy looking cottages, sheltering from the wind in some depression on a Yorkshire moor. Crowning all is the spacious roof, whereon are spent the stifling summer nights, while below it are the apartments for the *zanana*, screened from the gaze of the outer world by lace-like screens of perforated stone. Below these is the porch, with a small verandah at either side, wherein the master of the house may see his friends or transact his business, while the whole front is shaded by a series of *chajjas* [1] which, with the sun at meridian, will shade more than half the wall beneath them. Assuredly, this architecture and the individual features which characterise it are the true expression of Indian sentiment and of Indian genius.

The narrow streets of Bikanir, a city which, owing to its being in the centre of a mighty desert, has retained much of its old world character and individuality, might be compared to those of some mediaeval city of Europe. They are cool and shady ; neighbours can chat to each other from roof to roof across the street, while the entrances to the houses and their lower windows, all jealously closed, express all too vividly the intrigue and secrecy so dear to the Oriental mind. The local architecture, too, has received every encouragement at the hands of the present ruler. At Bhopal, a great mosque is springing into life, which will be a close rival to the Jami Masjid at Delhi, and, although many English architects are apt to be hard on such purely Indian work, here even the most narrow-minded of them could not but express his admiration. The presence of the moving spirit, Her Highness the Begam, behind the design, can be distinguished in the originality of the *zanana* gallery which, like the triforium of some mediaeval cathedral, runs along over the main arches of the façade, while at either end of the mosque are ladies' chapels. The whole treatment is nothing, if not original.

At Jaipur, the work of Lala Chiman Lall, the State Architect, calls for remark. His models for work on the new mausolea at Jaipur show originality and in his treatment of the newel and baluster is seen a happy combination of Eastern and Western ideas. Here is an Indian architect erecting, in his traditional style, buildings eminently adapted to the needs and customs of his people.

Some reasons for the inferior quality of the Indian architecture of British India have been suggested, and the problem remains to find a remedy for this inferiority and at the same time to prevent those parts of India, in which there are as yet no signs of decay, being affected by it. Genius will of course make its way without artificial stimulus, educational or otherwise, and it is for the assistance of average and low ability that a system of education must be designed. Until recently the average Indian has had to pick up what he can, and it is not to be wondered at that he has often inflicted on the public creations which only bear witness to his insufficient training. Draftsmanship occupies too prominent a place in his conception of architecture ; construction and practical modern considerations do not sufficiently control his designs. The same remark largely applies to the craftsman. Elaborately carved masonry is erected without any regard

[1] There is no term in English architecture which gives a successful rendering to this word. It is the projecting slab cornice which is seen on nearly every Indian building and which gives shade from the sun to windows or exposed wall surfaces.

to the principles of bond, and much of the profusely carved wood-work loses its charm owing to the only too obvious scamping of its 'mortise and tenon' jointing.

Sound planning and practical construction are more important than the façade and its ornament. It is much easier to copy than to think, and consequently the danger of dwelling too constantly on features of historical styles or adapting misunderstood European forms of design must be sedulously guarded against.

Excellent master craftsmen there are in plenty, but they cannot be brought directly under the influence of education, and it is for the architect to guide them.

GORDON SANDERSON.

June, 1911.

APPENDIX.

GOVERNMENT OF THE UNITED PROVINCES,

PUBLIC WORKS DEPARTMENT, BUILDINGS AND ROADS BRANCH.

No. 420/18CM, dated Allahabad, the 23rd March 1911.

From—The HON'BLE MR. C. E. V. GOUMENT, Secretary to Government,

To—The Superintendent, Muhammadan and British Monuments, Northern circle.

ORDERED that a copy of the following be forwarded for information and necessary action.

(Sd.) F. C. RICHARDSON,
Registrar,
For *Secretary.*

COPY of a letter No. 76, dated the 6th March 1911, from H. Sharp, Esq., Joint Secretary to the Government of India, Department of Education, (Archæology and Epigraphy), to the Secretary to the Government of the United Provinces, Public Works department.

Enclosures:—

Copy of the letter referred to with annexures.

No. 76, Calcutta, the 6th March 1911.

From—H. SHARP, ESQ., Joint Secretary to the Government of India,
Department of Education; Archæology and Epigraphy,

To—The Secretary to the Government of the United Provinces,
Public Works department.

SIR,—I am directed to enclose copy of a despatch from the Secretary of State for India,* forwarding a letter from the Executive Committee of the India Society in which it is suggested that Surveyors of the Archæological Department may be instructed to photograph, when on tour, any interesting types of modern Indian buildings and to note the names, adresses and local rates of remuneration of the principal craftsmen concerned in the design and decoration of such buildings. I am to request that, *with the permission of His Honour the Lieutenant-Governor, the Superintendent, Muhammadan and British Monuments, Northern circle*, may be asked to interest himself in, and report upon, the matter and that the *Local Government* will in due course report the result of such enquiry for the information of the Government of India.

*No. 108 (Revenue), dated the 16th December 1910, and enclosures.

I have the honour to be,
SIR,
Your most obedient servant,
H. SHARP,
Joint Secretary to the Government of India.

INDIA OFFICE, LONDON:
16th December 1910.

Revenue,
No. 108.

To His Excellency the Right Honourable the Governor General of India in Council.

MY LORD,

I FORWARD for the consideration of your Excellency's Government, and for any observations you may wish to make, a copy of a letter† from the Executive Committee of the India Society, in which it is suggested that, with a view to the collection of information regarding the principles and practice of present day architecture in India, the surveyors of the Archæological Department may be instructed to photograph, when on tour, any interesting type of modern Indian buildings and to note the names, addresses, and local rates of

Modern Indian architecture. Proposed inquiries by Archæological officers.

†Dated 20th November 1910, with three enclosures.

remuneration of the principal craftsmen concerned in the design and decoration of such buildings.

I have the honour to be,

MY LORD,

Your Lordship's most obedient servant,

CREWE.

ENCLOSURE.

INDIA SOCIETY TO INDIA OFFICE,

ARDEEVIN,

CHRIST CHURCH ROAD, HAMPSTEAD, N. W.:

20th November 1910.

SIR,—The Executive Committee of the India Society, which has been recently formed in London for the purpose of promoting the study and appreciation of Indian culture in all its aesthetic aspects, is anxious to obtain the support of the Government of India for the efforts it is making to collect material relating to the living traditions of Indian Art and Architecture.

2. To all artists, architects and art workers in Europe the fact that Indian art has an unbroken tradition of design and craftsmanship handed down from remote antiquity is a matter of even deeper interest than the magnificence of its ancient monuments; but whereas through the efforts of Government a great deal has been done of late years to assist archæological research, the importance of investigating the principles and practice of the living art and craft of India has not received anything like adequate attention.

3. The India Society is desirous of making a commencement in the latter direction by publishing photographic illustrations with notes of modern Indian architecture and architectural decoration. It is well known that there still exist all over India, especially in the Native States, a number of skilled master builders, descendants of the builders of the famous Hindu and Mughal Monuments, who continue to build temples, mosques, travellers' rest houses, and bathing tanks, &c., as well as domestic buildings, in the traditional styles of Indian Art. So great an authority as Fergusson has stated that he learned more from one of these men of the secrets of architectural art as practised in the Middle Ages than he had learnt from all the books he had read; and that, given the opportunities, they could even now rival the works of their forefathers.

The photograph enclosed of the doorway of a modern Hindu monastery at Puri, in Bengal, will give some idea of the high merits of this living architectural art.

4. It is unfortunately the case that owing to the spread of European fashions among the English-educated classes in India, and to departmental procedure in placing a very high premium upon the work of designers and craftsmen who merely imitate the commercial art of modern Europe, the number of these master builders is steadily diminishing and the quality of their work is deteriorating, so that India is gradually losing an invaluable part of her traditional art and craftsmanship. The India Society has not at present the means of undertaking on its own account a complete survey of living Indian architecture, but desires to draw the attention of the Government of India to the great importance of the subject, and would suggest that much valuable material could easily be collected at a trifling expense through the Archæological Department if the surveyors of the department were instructed, while on tour, to photograph interesting types of modern Indian buildings in the districts in which they are engaged, and to take notes of the names and addresses and local rates of remuneration of the principal craftsmen concerned in the designing and decoration of them. It is obvious that the historical continuity of Indian architectural traditions is a matter of the deepest interest to the student of archæology, and the information thus gained would also provide invaluable material for any official or non-official schemes for promoting technical and art education in India.

5. The Executive Committee is confident that the aims of the India Society will commend themselves to the Right Honourable the Secretary of State, and begs respectfully to suggest that this proposal may be forwarded for the favourable consideration of the Government of India.

A prospectus of the Society with the names of its members is submitted herewith for His Lordship's information.

I have &c.,
T. W. ROLLESTON,
Honorary Secretary, India Society.

To—The Under Secretary of State for India.

Enclosures :—

(1) Photographs of modern Indian architecture.

(2) Prospectus of India Society, with names of members.

Plate 2.

Photo.-Mechl. Dept., Thomason College, Roorkee.

DHARMSALA OF CHUNNA MAL, DELHI.

Plate 3.

DHARMSALA OF LACHMI NARAIN, DELHI.

Plate 4.

THE VARIOUS STAGES OF "*PIETRA DURA*" WORK, AGRA.

Plate 5.

Photo.-Mechl. Dept., Thomason College, Roorkee.

PUCHHEKARS AT WORK ON "*PIETRA DURA,*" AGRA.

Plate 6.

CARVING IN SOAP-STONE, AGRA.

Plate 7.

Photo -Mechl. Dept., Thomason College, Roorkee.

AT WORK ON A *JALI* SCREEN, AGRA.

Plate 8.

EXAMPLES FROM A PATTERN BOOK OF DRAWINGS, AGRA.

Plate 9

Photo.-Mechl. Dept., Thomason College, Roorkee.

THE BUILDERS OF THE DAOJI TEMPLE, AGRA.

Plate 10.

Photo.-Mechl. Dept., Thomason College, Roorkee.

THE DAOJI TEMPLE, AGRA.

Plate 11.

SAMADH OF SWAMIJI MAHARAJ, AGRA.

Plate 12.

Photo,-Mechl. Dept., Thomason College, Roorkee.

SAMADH OF SWAMIJI MAHARAJ, AGRA.

Photo.-Mechl. Dept., Thomason College, Roorkee.

***SAMADH* OF SWAMIJI MAHARAJ, AGRA.**

DRAWING OF A CORNER *CHATTRI.*

Plate 14.

A MODERN HOUSE, ALLAHABAD.

Plate 15.

Photo.-Mechl. Dept., Thomason College, Roorkee.

A MODERN HOUSE, ALLAHABAD.

Plate 16.

THE NUDWAT—UL—ULAMA, LUCKNOW.
FROM S. W.

Plate 17.

Photo.-Mechl. Dept., Thomason College, Roorkee.

THE NUDWAT—UL—ULAMA, LUCKNOW.
FROM N. E.

Plate 18.

A MODERN HOUSE, AJMER.

Plate 19.

Photo.-Mechl. Dept., Thomason College, Roorkee.

A MODERN HOUSE, AJMER.

Plate 20.

A MODERN HOUSE, AJMER.

Plate 21.

Photo.-Mechl. Dept., Thomason College, Roorkee.

THE HOUSE OF RAI BAHADUR SETH SOBHAG MAL, AJMER.

Plate 22.

THE ARYA SAMAJ PRESS, AJMER.

Plate 23.

Photo.-Mechl. Dept., Thomason College, Roorkee.

MARBLE *CHATTRI* IN SARAOJI'S GARDEN.

Plate 24.

Photo.-Mechl. Dept., Thomason College, Roorkee.

DRAWING OF THE TAJ-UL-MASAJID, BHOPAL.

Plate 25.

THE TAJ-UL-MASAJID, BHOPAL

Plate 26

Photo.-Mechl. Dept., Thomason College, Roorkee.

THE TAJ-UL-MASAJID, BHOPAL.
VIEW OF COURTYARD.

Plate 27.

THE TAJ-UL-MASAJID, BHOPAL.
EAST GATE UNDER CONSTRUCTION.

Plate 28.

Photo.-Mechl. Dept., Thomason College, Roorkee.

THE TAJ-UL-MASAJID, BHOPAL.
ZANANA GALLERY.

Plate 29.

Photo.-Mechl. Dept., Thomason College, Roorkee.

THE TAJ-UL-MASAJID, BHOPAL.
A STONE FOR DRUM OF THE DOME.

Plate 30.

THE TAJ-UL-MASAJID, BHOPAL.
A CORNER *CHATTRI.*

Plate 31.

KULSUM BI'S MOSQUE, BHOPAL.

Plate 32.

Photo.-Mechl. Dept., Thomason College, Roorkee.

THE SHAUKAT MAHAL, BHOPAL.

Plate 33.

MOTI MAL'S HOUSE, BIKANIR.

Plate 34.

Photo.-Mechl. Dept., Thomason College, Roorkee.

MOTI MAL'S HOUSE, BIKANIR.

Plate 35.

Photo.-Mechl. Dept., Thomason College. Roorkee.

A TYPICAL FACADE, BIKANIR.

Plate 36.

MEHTA STREET, BIKANIR.

Plate 37.

Photo.-Mechl. Dept., Thomason College, Roorkee.

A MODERN HOUSE, BIKANIR.

Plate 38.

PANNA LALL'S MANDIR, BIKANIR.

Plate 39.

A MODERN HOUSE, BIKANIR.

Plate 40.

Photo.-Mechl. Dept., Thomason College, Roorkee.

AN INTERIOR, BIKANIR.

Plate 41.

Photo.-Mechl. Dept., Thomason College. Roorkee.

THE DARGAH MANDIR, BIKANIR.

Plate 42.

MAUSOLEA AT DEVI KUND, BIKANIR.

Plate 43.

TEMPLE OF SAIDA SUHK, BIKANIR.

Plate 44.

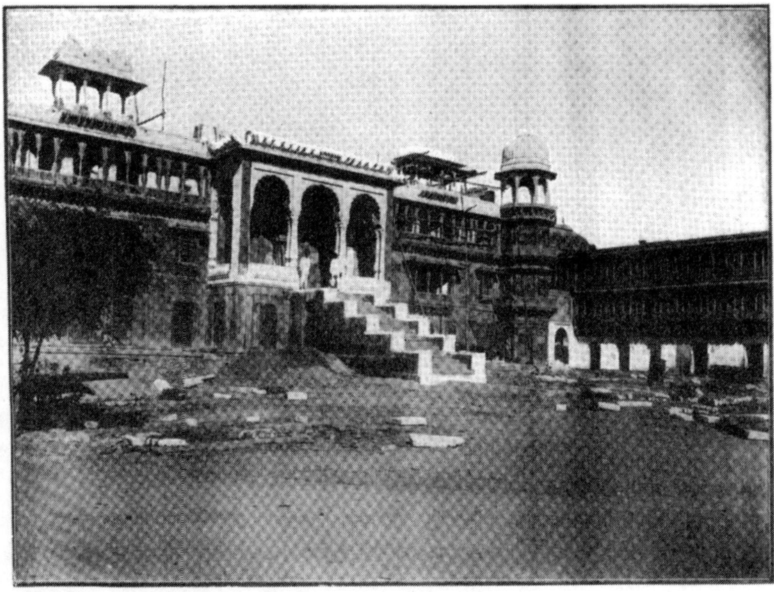

Photo.-Mechl. Dept., Thomason College, Roorkee.

RATI BIHARI'S TEMPLE, BIKANIR.
(UNDER CONSTRUCTION).

Plate 45.

NEW TEAK DOOR, OLD PALACE, BIKANIR.

Plate 46.

Photo.-Mechl. Dept., Thomason College, Roorkee.

CARPENTERS AT WORK, OLD PALACE, BIKANIR.

Plate 47.

Photo.-Mechl. Dept., Thomason College, Roorkee.

OLD DOOR AT HOUSE OF SRI KRISHAN DAS, BIKANIR.

Plate 48.

SILVER DOOR. OLD PALACE, BIKANIR.

Plate 49.

FACADE, OLD PALACE, BIKANIR.

Plate 50.

Photo.-Mechl. Dept., Thomason College, Roorkee.

INTERIOR ROOMS, OLD PALACE, BIKANIR.

Plate 51.

INTERIOR ROOMS, OLD PALACE, BIKANIR.

Plate 52.

Photo.-Mechl. Dept., Thomason College, Roorkee.

COURTYARD OF OLD PALACE, BIKANIR.
(UNDER REPAIR).

Plate 53.

NEW DARBAR HALL: OLD PALACE, BIKANIR.

Plate 54.

Photo.-Mechl. Dept., Thomason College, Roorkee.

COURTYARD OF NEW DARBAR HALL: OLD PALACE, BIKANIR.

Photo.-Mechl. Dept. Thomason College, Roorkee.

OLD PALACE, BIKANIR.
ENTRANCE TO NEW DARBAR HALL.

Plate 56.

Photo.-Mechl. Dept., Thomason College, Roorkee.

OLD PALACE, BIKANIR.
INTERIOR OF NEW DARBAR HALL.

Photo.-Mechl. Depth., Thomason College, Roorkee.

OLD PALACE, BIKANIR.
INTERIOR OF NEW DARBAR HALL.

Plate 58.

Photo.-Mechl. Dept. Thomason College, Roorkee.

OLD PALACE, BIKANIR.
INTERIOR OF NEW DARBAR HALL.

Plate 59.

Photo.-Mechl. Dept., Thomason College, Roorkee.

A TYPICAL HOUSE, GWALIOR.

Plate 60.

A TYPICAL HOUSE, GWALIOR.

Plate 61.

Photo.-Mechl. Dept., Thomason College, Roorkee.

A PROJECTING BALCONY, GWALOIR.

Plate 62.

GIRDHARI MAL'S HOUSE, GWALIOR.

Plate 63.

ARCADING AT STREET SIDE, GWALIOR.

Plate 64.

Photo.-Mechl. Dept., Thomason College, Roorkee.

CHATTRI OF DAULAT RAO MAHARAJ, GWALIOR.

Plate 65.

CHATTRI OF DAULAT RAO MAHARAJ, GWALIOR.
DETAIL OF CARVING.

Plate 66.

Photo.-Mechl. Dept., Thomason College, Roorkee.

CHATTRI OF DAULAT RAO MAHARAJ, GWALIOR.
INTERIOR.

Plate 67.

GUEST HOUSE, THE PALACE, JAIPUR.
DESIGNED BY LALA CHIMAN LAL, STATE ARCHITECT.

Plate 68.

Photo.-Mechl. Dept, Thomason College, Roorkee.

GUEST HOUSE, THE PALACE, JAIPUR.

Plate 69.

NEW ROYAL MAUSOLEUM, JAIPUR.

Plate 70.

Photo.-Mechl. Dept., Thomason College, Roorkee.

ENTRANCE TO NEW ROYAL MAUSOLEUM, JAIPUR.

Photo,-Mechl. Depth. Thomason College, Roorkee

INTERIOR OF NEW ROYAL MAUSOLEUM,JAIPUR.

Plate 72.

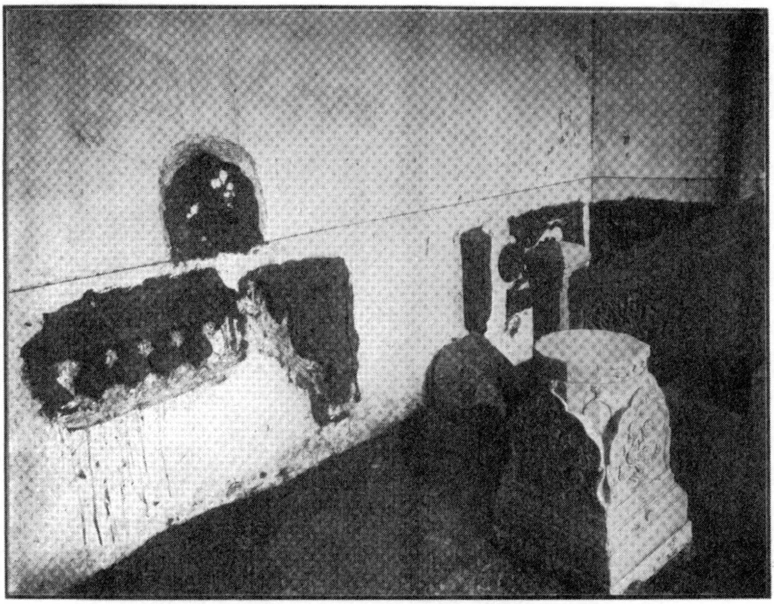

CLAY MODELS, NEW ROYAL MAUSOLEUM, JAIPUR.

Plate 73.

Photo.-Mechl. Dept., Thomason College, Roorkee.

NEW ROYAL MAUSOLEUM, JAIPUR.

ERECTION OF CLAY MODELS ON AN EXISTING *CHATTRI*.

Plate 74.

Photo.-Mechl. Dept., Thomason College, Roorkee.

DAROGAJI'S HOUSE, JAIPUR.

Plate 75.

INTERIOR OF DAROGAJI'S HOUSE, JAIPUR.

Plate 76.

JAIPUR—ISHA NANA'S HOUSE.

Plate 77.

Photo-Mechl. Dept., Thomason College, Roorkee.

A STREET CORNER, JAIPUR.

Plate 78.

TYPICAL STREET ARCHITECTURE, JAIPUR.

Plate 79.

Photo.-Mechl. Dept., Thomason College, Roorkee.

AN INTERIOR, JAIPUR.

Plate 80.

THE PALACE BUILDINGS, JODHPUR FORT.

Plate 81.

Photo.-Mechl. Dept., Thomason College, Roorkee.

THE PALACE BUILDINGS, JODHPUR FORT.

Plate 82.

Photo.-Mechl. Dept., Thomason College, Roorkee.

THE PALACE BUILDINGS, JODHPUR FORT.

Plate 83.

THE PALACE BUILDINGS, JODHPUR FORT.

Plate 84.

JODHPUR FORT. THE PALACE BUILDINGS.

Plate 85.

Photo.-Mechl. Dept., Thomason College, Roorkee.

JODHPUR. THE OLD PALACE OF MAHARAJ SUR SINGH.

Plate 86.

THE RANSURJI KA MANDIR, JODHPUR.

Plate 87

Photo-Mechl. Dept., Thomason College Roorkee.

SHOPS NEAR THE RANSURJI KA MANDIR, JODHPUR.

Plate 88.

Photo.-Mechl. Dept., Thomason College, Roorkee.

TEMPLE OF RAJ GOPAL, JODHPUR.

Plate 89.

NEW COURTS, JODHPUR.

Plate 90.

Photo.-Mechl. Dept., Thomason College, Roorkee.

A TYPICAL HOUSE, UDAIPUR.

Plate 91.

TYPE OF GATEWAY, UDAIPUR.

Plate 92.

TYPE OF GATEWAY, UDAIPUR.

Plate 93.

Photo.-Mechl. Dept., Thomason College, Roorkee.

AN ARCADED STREET, UDAIPUR.